to QUILTING
Tips & Tricks

by Penny Haren

Landauer Publishing

Copyright © 2020 by Penny Haren and Landauer Publishing
(*www.landauerpub.com*), an imprint of
Fox Chapel Publishing Company, Inc.,
903 Square Street, Mount Joy, PA 17552.

Shutterstock credits for front cover: Iryna Kalamurza (bottom far left);
MaxCab (center, bottom middle left); melnikof (bottom middle right);
SunCity (bottom far right)

ISBN: 978-1-947163-53-9

Printed in Canada
First printing

Contents

Introduction

Whether your sewing room is large or small, if you take the time to organize both your space and your supplies, you'll have a much easier time when you're ready to sew.

So let's get that sewing room organized! Regardless of your skill level, these quilting tips and tricks will make your quilting faster, easier, and better!

I'm sharing some of my tried and true quilting tips and tricks in this handy pocket guide. From keeping your supplies clean to making design boards and so much more!

I'll help you find ways to organize your sewing room to keep everything ready for your next quilt project. You will love these thread, tool, and fabric storage ideas as well as design organization and displays.

Penny
Newark, Ohio

Author of:
Penny Haren's Pieced Appliqué Blocks Made Easy
Penny Haren's Pieced Appliqué More Blocks & Projects
Penny Haren's Pieced Appliqué Weekend Projects
Penny Haren's Pieced Appliqué Blocks Made Easy
Quilt Block Fusion
Log Cabin Quilts

Organizing Your Space

1 Hanging Projects

Many of us have a closet in our sewing room. Hang your projects on the rod in vinyl mesh bags with "S" hooks. These bags come in a variety of sizes—large enough to hold a book and everything you need to make the project. You can literally hang over 100 projects vertically—easy to see and easy to find!

2 Folding Tables

If you use folding tables in your sewing room, consider two 4' (1.22m) tables instead of an 8' (2.44m) table. The shorter length makes it more stable and less likely to vibrate when sewing.

3 Cutting Tables

Design your cutting table so that it is the appropriate height for you. Kitchen counter height is ideal for someone who is of average height—approximately 5' 4" (1.63m) for women. Adjust accordingly.

Organizing Your Space

4 Stash

Organize your stash by type rather than color. Then when you are ready to make a scrappy project, simply pull out the bin of country fabrics, batiks, brights, backgrounds, Asian prints, pastels, etc. and start cutting. Everything in the bin will go together!

5 Background Fabric

If you are uncomfortable choosing fabrics for scrap quilts, use the same background fabric for the entire quilt. It gives your eyes a place to rest and gives a more controlled look.

6 Distributing Colors Evenly

When making scrap quilts over a period of time—and in my case, sometimes years—wait to put the blocks together so that the colors will be distributed evenly throughout the quilt. The shades of popular colors change from year to year. (Moss green is popular one year, evergreen the next.)

Sewing Machine

7 Buy from a Local Dealer

When buying a sewing machine, buy it from a reputable local dealer who also services machines. Then when you have a question or want to learn how to use all of those bells and whistles, the support is there.

8 Marking Your Machine

You own your sewing machine so you can deface it! When I have my machine serviced and the stitch is perfect, I mark the tension guides as the "default." Have a favorite width for machine appliqué? Mark it with a permanent marker in an inconspicuous place.

Sewing Machine

9 Threading

Having trouble threading a machine needle? Switch to a jean needle. It has a larger eye to accommodate heavier weight jean thread and has a sharp point so it works well for traditional piecing.

10 Microtex Needles

When topstitching, machine appliquéing, or embroidering, use a Microtex needle. These needles have a very sharp, fine point. When sewing fusibles, use a non-stick needle. They come in different sizes and won't "gunk up" while sewing.

11 Sewing with Kids

When sewing with children, set up the sewing machine so it works for their size. Use a children's table or raise the foot pedal by placing it on a box or crate.

Rotary Cutting Mats

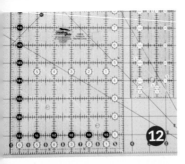

12 Match the Lines

Place a ruler on the gridded side of your cutting mat. If the marks on the ruler line up with the lines on the cutting mat, it is okay to use cutting mat markings as guides when rotary cutting.

- - - - - - - - - - - - - - - - - - - -

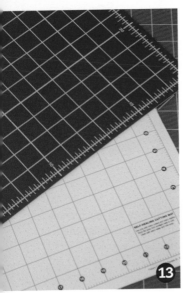

13 Grid Lines

If using the grid lines on your rotary cutting mat, utilize the horizontal AND vertical lines. Cut strips to the appropriate width by using the vertical lines on the mat, then cut squares or rectangles by sub-cutting using the horizontal lines.

Rotary Cutting Mats

14 Multiple Cuts

If you are making multiple cuts of the same fabric and using the grids on the rotary cutting mat, mark the top and bottom of the cutting lines with a water soluble marker. For instance, if you are cutting 3½" (8.89cm) strips, mark the 3½" (8.89cm), 7" (17.78cm), 10½" (26.67cm), and 14" (35.56cm) grid lines. When done, simply wash away the markings with a damp cloth.

15 Place your Mat on a Corner

If you place your cutting mat on the corner of your cutting table. Then you can rotate your body instead of the block to cut all sides of a block when trimming.

16 Consider the Cutting Area

Consider the area where you rotary cut before buying a mat. Many of us would love a 24" x 36" (60.96 x 91.44cm) mat—but if you cut on a kitchen counter that is a standard 21" (53.34cm) depth, the mat won't fit! And, if you have a petite stature, you may not be able to apply pressure the entire height of the board. An 18" x 24" (45.72 x 60.96cm) mat may be a better option.

17 Mat Storing

Store your mat flat and keep it out of the sun to eliminate warping. Limited space? Consider storing it between a mattress and box spring.

Rotary Cutting Mats

18 Cutting Mat Life

Use the unmarked side of the mat when you don't need grid lines—such as when you are trimming blocks. It will extend the life of your cutting mat.

19 Cleaning Your Mat

Use a rubber eraser to clean your rotary cutting mat. When cutting fabrics—especially flannel, fleece, and Cuddle® fabrics, fibers become embedded in the cuts made with the rotary cutter so the mat can't "heal." A rubber eraser removes all of these fibers so the mat will last much longer.

Cutting

20 Reduce Cutting Time

If you are cutting out two layers of fabric at a time and I am cutting out eight, it will take you four times longer to cut out your quilt. Do the math: It will take you four hours to cut out what I can cut in one hour which means I have already been sewing for three hours!

21 Stack Strip Sets

When sub-cutting eight layers at time, be sure to stack your strips on the mat. By stacking six sets of eight 2½" (6.35cm) strips on your mat, for instance, you can cut out 48 pieces every time you move your ruler!

Cutting

22 Trimming and Cutting

A 60mm blade is the perfect choice for trimming quilts and cutting thicker fabrics, such as flannels, Cuddle fabrics, and fleeces.

23 Replace Your Cutting Blade

Replace your rotary cutting blade when needed. You should easily be able to cut eight layers of fabric at a time. If you can't, it is time to replace your blade.

24 Have Replacement Blades on Hand

Consider the circumference of a rotary cutting blade. A 28mm blade will need to be replaced more often than a 60mm blade, so plan accordingly and have replacement blades on hand.

Cutting

25 Save the Packaging

Save the packaging when buying rotary cutting blades. Use it to dispose of the old blades safely.

26 Pinning Your Layers to Cut

When cutting multiple layers that will then be sub-cut, pin them together along the length of the strips. The pins stop the fabric from shifting as the smaller units are cut. Remove the pins as needed.

Cutting

27 Create Your Own Precuts

Save money by creating your own precuts. Cut your collection of fat quarters into three strips the width of the fat quarter: a 10" (25.40cm) strip (sub-cut into two 10" (25.40cm) squares); a 5" (12.70cm) strip (sub-cut into four 5" (12.70cm) squares); and a 2½" (6.35cm) strip.

28 Donate Your Scraps

Have an extra wastebasket near your cutting station with a plastic bag in it. When you are cutting fabrics and create scraps that you know you will not use, put them in the basket. When the bag is full, remove it and donate the scraps to someone who will use them!

Cutting

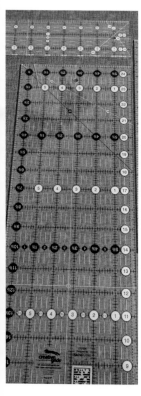

29 Rectangle Ruler

Choose rectangular rulers that feature a center line. When trimming blocks such as four patches, this center line can be placed on the seam line for trimming—and the additional length is easier to hold. The center line can also be used to cut ¼" (0.64cm) strips. For instance, if you need 1¼" (3.18cm) cuts, use the center line on a 2½" (6.35cm) rectangle; 1¾" (4.46cm) cuts, use the center line on a 3½" (8.89cm) rectangle; etc.

30 18½" (47cm)–
Long Ruler

Consider buying rectangular rulers that are 18½" (47cm) long, especially if your mat is 18" x 24" (46 x 61cm) which is the most popular size. They will still span an 18" x 24" (46 x 61cm) mat, are easier to manipulate, and cost less. Besides, many of us may find it difficult to apply pressure the entire length of a longer ruler to cut anyway!

Notions

31 Quality Notions

Buy quality notions. A few dollars means the difference between a seam ripper with a fine point that can fit between the stitches and a grip that fits your hand—and one that doesn't. Quality can last a lifetime!

32 Leftover Threads

Use up partial spools of threads and bobbins to piece scrap quilts. Since the fabrics are a combination of all colors, a variety of thread colors will blend nicely and is a great money saver!

33 Numbered Pins

Make your own numbered pins from flower head pins. Mark the flower head with a fine point marker. Then use these numbered pins to mark rows, blocks, or pieces in a paper-pieced pattern.

Notions

34 Magnetic Pin Holders

With the popularity of magnetic pin holders, be sure to buy pins that are magnetic—which means they must be made from iron or nickel.

35 Storing Water-Based Notions

Store water-based notions such as glue sticks and water-soluble markers in the refrigerator. The moist environment will keep them fresh for months.

36 Glue Sticks

Water-soluble glue sticks—the white kind you ate in kindergarten—are reasonably priced and work well with fabric. Look for the brands that say "machine washable."

37 Bobbin Saver

Wind bobbins with matching threads for your handwork. A bobbin saver holds up to 20 bobbins and fits around them snuggly so they don't unwind.

Picking a Project

38 Read before You Buy

Read the entire pattern before you buy fabric and commit to a quilt. If the instructions tell you to cut 640 squares to make four-patches, there is obviously a better way to do it or you may want to rethink your pattern choice. Anyone can write a pattern. That does not mean they can do it well or know the tips and tricks to make it easier.

39 Test the Pattern

Before investing the time and money into a queen- or king-size quilt, test the block or pattern by making a smaller version that can then be completed as a floor pillow. Then you will know if you want to make it 16 more times— the equivalent of a queen or king size quilt!

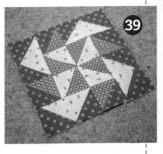

Picking a Project

40 Play with Color Copies

Save time and money when designing a quilt. Run color copies of an actual sample block. Play with the color copies until you have a design that is pleasing to your eye; *then* cut the fabric and make the project.

41 Choosing Exchange Blocks

When choosing blocks for friendship exchanges or joint projects, choose blocks that can all be trimmed to a standard size. Half-square triangles and four-patches for instance can be cut larger and trimmed to the same size after sewing. Seam allowance is no longer an issue and everyone can participate!

41

Picking a Project

42 Dresden Plates

Has a Dresden Plate quilt caught your eye? Count the number of petals in the plates and divide 360° by that number to determine the angled ruler you would need. For instance, a 12 petal Dresden Plate is made with a 30 degree ruler (360 divided by 12).

Pattern from *Classic to Contemporary String Quilts* by Mary M. Hogan available at Fox Chapel Publishing (*www.foxchapelpublishing.com*)

43 Choosing a Quilt

When choosing a quilt, consider the time involved. That border with over 400 appliquéd leaves may be stunning—but will it turn into a UFO and stop you from finishing the quilt? Will a simpler pieced border be just as effective? The choice is yours.

44 Plan the Size of your Quilt

When making a quilt, don't assume that it will fit your bed. Although the mattress sizes are standard, the height of a mattress, box springs, and pillow tops are not—so plan ahead. Place a flat sheet on the bed so that it drops on both sides and the end where you want it. Add a few inches (centimeters) to allow for the shrinkage that occurs when quilting—approximately 1 (2.54cm) to 2 (5.08cm) inches per yard. Adjust the pattern accordingly.

Picking a Project

45 Set Your Table First

When making a table runner for your table, set the table first. And then measure the size that would look best. Most patterns can be easily adapted to your needs by reducing the width of a border, eliminating a row of blocks, etc.

Choosing Fabric

46 Directional Prints

When choosing fabrics for a project, be aware of directional prints. You may have to cut them one layer at a time to retain the design. Make sure it is worth it!

----

47 Matching Print Designs

Directional prints and stripes can be dramatic when used in curtains and bed skirts. Check to be sure that the design can be matched when piecing strips together—similar to hanging wallpaper. Not all fabrics are printed this way so buy accordingly.

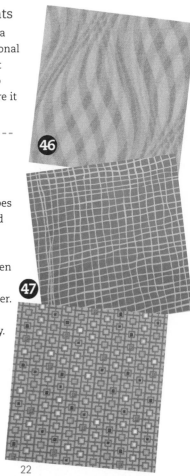

Choosing Fabric

48 Take Pictures of your Block Layout

When laying out the blocks for a quilt, take pictures with your phone. Then you can play with different block placements and choose your favorites. Added bonus? Once you start sewing it together, you have a visual of the entire project if you need it!

49 Quilt Shop Fabric Quality

When buying fabric, look for quilt shop quality lines. The thread count is higher than cheaper fabrics and will last longer.

50 Use the Same Fabric Quality

Don't include different qualities of fabrics in the same quilt. A quilt is only as good as its lowest quality fabric. When that fabric wears out, the quilt is history.

49

Borders

51 Measure in Several Places

When adding borders, measure the length and width of the quilt in several places and then cut the border to that measurement.

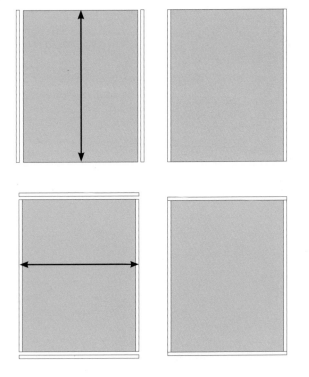

Borders

52 Cutting the Length of the Fabric

Cutting borders parallel to the selvage means that they can be cut without piecing. An added bonus? There is absolutely no stretch to the length of the fabric so cutting borders the length of the fabric is a great way to stabilize quilts that are set on point.

53 Reduce Your Stitch Length

When creating Rail Fence borders or other borders with lots of seams on the outer edge, reduce your stitch length. The reduced stitch length will stop these seams from coming apart while machine quilting.

⎯ ⎯ ⎯ ⎯ ⎯ ⎯
long stitch

⎯ ⎯ ⎯ ⎯ ⎯ ⎯ ⎯
medium stitch

- - - - - - - - - - - - - - - -
short stitch

54 Look at the Shadow Through

When choosing a background fabric, consider shadow through. Red and white quilts are beautiful, for instance, but red threads and seams may show on the front of the quilt. Clip threads and trim seams accordingly, and try to press seams toward the darker fabrics when possible.

Choosing Backing

55 Choose Cuddle for Kids

Want to make children smile? Back their quilts with a Cuddle-type fabric and then make matching Cuddle pillowcases.

- -

56 No Fabric Waste

Before piecing a quilt, consider the backing. There are many wonderful 60"–62" (152.40–157.48cm)–wide backings available—from Cuddle-type fabrics to Kona cotton. By keeping the width of throws and twin quilts to 55"–57" (139.70–144.78cm), the backing will not have to be pieced and there will be no waste of fabric.

- -

57 Buy by the Bolt

Consider buying backing fabric by the bolt. Many shops will give a discount if you buy an entire bolt, so I buy 60" (152.40cm)–wide Cuddle-type fabrics in a neutral color. Many come on 12 (10.97m) yard bolts which is enough to back approximately four twin sized quilts.

Pressing

58 Ironing Surface Matters

Consider pressing on a 100% wool mat. The wool absorbs the seams and the fabric doesn't slide as it does on a heat resistant surface.

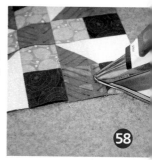

59 Stop Distortion and Stretching

When pressing strip sets, pull the fabric slightly from selvage to selvage (left to right). This slight tension will stop the fabric from distorting and stretching from top to bottom.

60 When to Press Seams Open

Don't be afraid to press seams open. Pressing seams open distributes the fabric evenly and stops darker fabrics from shadowing through. It is the obvious choice when working in miniature.

Appliqué & Embroidery

61 Sewing on Buttons

Make short work when sewing on buttons by using #8 pearl cotton. It is the equivalent of six strands of thread, so it is very strong and sturdy.

62 Consider Batiks

Consider using batiks when turning small appliqué pieces. Because of the manufacturing process, it is thin and tightly woven—which means it is easy to turn and frays very little.

63 Machine Baste Pieces in Place

When hand appliquéing, machine baste the pieces in place so they don't come off when working on the piece and traveling. Remove the basting stitches as each piece is completed so you know exactly how much you have accomplished.

Appliqué & Embroidery

64 Tracing Redwork

When tracing a redwork design, iron freezer paper to the wrong side of the fabric to stabilize it. Then use a light box and a fine-point red marker to trace the design. Any markings that are not covered will blend in with the embroidery thread and not show.

Pattern from *Simply Redwork* by Helen Stubbings available at Fox Chapel Publishing (*www.foxchapelpublishing.com*)

65 Multiple Templates

Cut multiple templates at one time by stapling layers of paper together. Turn the button in the base of the stapler to create temporary staples. The points of the staples will point out instead of in and can be removed with a fingernail.

66 Freezer Paper Stabilizes Wool

Rough cut around the freezer paper templates for wool appliqués. Then press the freezer paper to the wool before cutting to the actual shape. The freezer paper stabilizes the wool and makes it easier to cut. Glue the wool appliqués in place on the background fabric before removing the paper.

Machine Quilting

67 Schedule with Your Machine Quilter

When planning a quilt, call the machine quilter and schedule a realistic time to have it quilted. Many machine quilters are booked months in advance, so plan accordingly. This also gives you a self-imposed deadline to finish that quilt top!

68 Talk with Your Machine Quilter

Ask your machine quilter how they would like your quilt prepped for machine quilting. Most require the backing to be 3" (7.62cm) wider on all sides so they can attach it to the machine. They may also prefer specific battings. Respect their wishes!

69 Combine Seasons

When quilting table runners and place mats, use a decorative fabric on the back as well. It can even be a different season since the only fabric the front and back of the project "share" is the binding, for instance, a red binding to coordinate with the front of a Christmas runner can showcase a Valentine's Day fabric backing.

69

Machine Quilting

70 Press and Clip Your Quilt Top

When preparing a quilt top for quilting, press the quilt from the back to ensure that the seams are where you want them to be. Clip threads that could shadow through on lighter backgrounds. Then press and clip threads from the front.

71 Protective Batting for Hot Dishes

Use a batting such as Insul-Bright® in place mats and table runners. They can then be used in place of trivets to protect your table when serving hot dishes.

72 Fleece Backing

Consider using a quilt shop quality fleece on the back of a quilt. Since it is double sided, you don't need to use batting, which can be a huge money saver. And, since it is at least 60" (152.40cm)–wide, it is the perfect choice for a children's throw or bed quilt. Very warm and virtually indestructible!

Machine Quilting

73 Use Scraps of Batting

Use scraps of batting in smaller projects. The scraps of batting can be fused together with a product such as Heat Press Batting Together™—which is a fusible tape available in a variety of widths.

74 Heat Press Batting Together

When working on a number of smaller projects, use Heat Press Batting Together. Lay the pieces right side down on an ironing board. Butt the raw edges together and fuse them with the tape. They can then be machine quilted as one piece—and cut apart after quilting to preserve the seam allowance. Bonus? There is only one setup charge from the machine quilter!

Machine Quilting

75 Soft and Stable™

Use a product such as Soft and Stable in place of batting when quilting wall hangings. It has more body so the wall hanging will lay flat and the machine quilting shows beautifully.

76 Saving for Quality Machine Quilting

Custom machine quilting can be expensive—but is worth every penny and can literally turn an okay quilt into a work of art. When working on an heirloom quality or block of the month quilt, set aside money each month as you work on the blocks. Then, when the quilt is done, you'll have the money to machine quilt it the way you want!

77 Machine Quilt Gift Certificates

Ask your family for machine quilting gift certificates from your favorite longarmer. This is a gift you will definitely appreciate and use!

Binding

78 Scrap Binding

Save scraps of binding. When making scrap quilts, piece these scraps together to bind the quilt. Who doesn't love a free binding?

79 Sew and Flip from Back to Front

When binding quilts with a plush backing such as Minkee® or Cuddle, consider sewing the binding to the back of the quilt and flipping it to the top for the hand-stitching. That way you will be needling through the cotton fabric instead of a textured nap.

Binding

80 Bias Binding Lasts Longer

Bias binding lasts longer. Think about it: If you cut fabric strips for binding on the straight of grain, the same thread is on the outside edge of the quilt and will wear away quickly. If the fabric is cut on the bias, that wear will be distributed over 65 threads per 1" (2.54cm) so if one thread breaks, you still have 64 other threads in place!

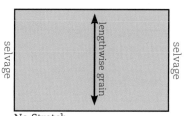

No Stretch

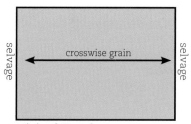

Minimal Stretch

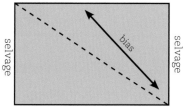

Maximum Stretch

Binding

81 Alleviate Bulk

Piece binding strips on the diagonal to alleviate bulk. If you sew vertical seams and press those seams to one side, you will have three layers of fabric on the seam side. By the time the binding is sewn to the quilt, multiply that by three: NINE layers of fabric at each seam means you just created a chew toy for a dog!

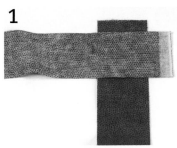

Position binding strips to mark and sew them together using the catch-phrase "ho-down," by placing the horizontal strip face down on top of the vertical strip that's face up.

Sew the binding strips together on the drawn line to create a diagonal seam.

Binding

Trim the seam
and press open.

Press a 45°
diagonal fold at
the beginning end
of the binding strip.

With wrong sides
together, fold and
press the entire length
of the binding strip
in half.

82 Scraps for Coordinating Accessories

Use the scraps of fabric from a project to make coordinating accessories for the room. Making a bed quilt? Why not make a table runner for the dresser or a storage case for jewelry or matching pillows . . . you get the idea!

Decorating

83 Consider the Extras

When making a quilt, consider where it will be used. Should you buy extra fabric for curtains? A bed skirt? Matching pillowcases? Get it now! Your favorite print may be discontinued by the time the quilt is done.

84 Pillowcases

Make pillowcases to match your bed-sized quilts. They take less than 30 minutes, require a yard (meter) of fabric, and add that Martha Stewart touch to the room. Added bonus? When the quilt is not in use, store it in the pillowcase. The pillowcase protects the quilt and makes it instantly recognizable when stored in the linen closet.

84

Decorating

85 Sleeves on Top and Bottom

When hanging a quilt, sew a sleeve to the top and bottom of the quilt. Rotate the quilt occasionally so that the same areas of the quilt aren't always exposed to the light. Place a rod in both the top and bottom sleeves. They act as stretcher bars and the quilt will lay flat.

86 Decorative Quilt Displays

Display quilts creatively. Hang a quilt hanger clamp or decorative curtain rod quilt hanger clamp to hang a coordinating quilt on the wall. This is a great way to add a lovely accent to a guest room. Also, if your guests are cold, another quilt is always within easy reach.

Decorating

87 Adding Charm to Any Room

Add charm to any room by adding quilts, blocks, and miniature quilts in creative ways. Staple them over a canvas. Hang an empty decorative frame over them so that the wall shows through as a border. Or attach a quilt so it shows through the sashings in an old window. Think outside of the box!

88 Quilting Shadow Box

Inherited some quilting supplies and blocks? Why not display them in a shadow box? A block that grandma pieced is displayed nicely when combined with some of her wooden spools and antique scissors. Include a picture of her to make your heart sing.

Decorating

89 Use the Back of the Quilt or Table Runner

Quilts and table runners make beautiful tablecloths. If you want to actually eat on the quilt or table runner, turn it over to showcase a beautiful backing. Then if someone spills something, it won't stain the front. And if a child spills his drink, the quilt will absorb it—no harm no foul!

Decorating

90 Easy Foot Stool

Cut a 22" (55.88cm) square of plywood and round the corners, and add four wooden legs to this base. It's a great way to stack the pillows when they aren't being used. A wonderful gift at a minimal cost—and the pillows are a good way to use up scraps!

91 Floor Pillows

A set of three 24" (60.96cm) floor pillows make a great gift! Display all three across the length of a twin-size bed pushed against a wall to turn it into an instant couch. Choose their school colors or showcase a beloved T-shirt!

Miscellaneous

92 Quilted Holiday Gifts

Give quilted stockings for a wedding shower gift. The couple will love receiving their first holiday decorations. Then make a matching tree skirt for the wedding gift. Save some of the fabric to make matching stockings when you are invited to the baby shower and you'll look like Martha Stewart!

93 Include Washing Instructions

Include washing instructions and a phosphate-free laundry soap such as Soak® whenever you gift a quilt—a gentle reminder to treat this gift with love and care!

Miscellaneous

94 Mending an Old Quilt

Need to mend an old quilt? Run a color copy of the largest section of that print in the quilt. Then transfer that print to fabric using your favorite brand of printable fabric sheets. This fabric will be faded like the original and blend right in.

95 #8 Pigma Micron Pen

Use a #8 Pigma Micron Pen to write on a quilt. The tip is thick so you can write on fabric just like you would on paper.

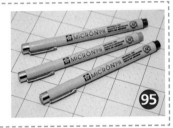

96 Pins as Arrows

Always pin together the fabric so the point of the pin acts like an arrow, pointing to the side of the block that needs sewn.

Miscellaneous

97 Paper Plates Help with Multiple Blocks

When paper-piecing, cut out all of the fabric for each block and place them on a paper-plate with the main fabric on top. Save time by working on multiple blocks at once—each on its own plate. Sew all of the blocks, press, trim, and repeat.

98 Center Prairie Points

To fussy cut prairie points, center a design in a quarter of a square. When the square is folded, the design will be centered on the prairie point.

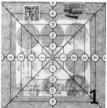

Cut a square with the design centered

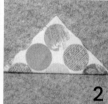

Fold the square from corner to corner

Fold the triangle from corner to corner

99 Glue instead of a Pin

When matching seams, use a dab of glue instead of a pin. The fabric won't shift while sewing so the seams will match when sewn together.

Miscellaneous

100 Avoiding Bias Edges

Avoid bias edges on the outside edge of a quilt. If blocks are set on point, the side setting triangles should be cut from squares cut both ways on the diagonal so the long edge is on the straight of grain. The corner triangles should be cut once on the diagonal so both outside edges are on the straight of grain.

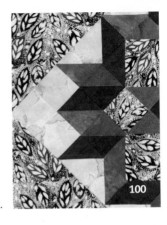

101 Stabilize First

T-shirts or other stretchy fabrics can be incorporated into a memory quilt if they are stabilized first. Simply iron on a fusible tricot, which will stop the knit from stretching so it can be sewn like any other fabric. Be sure to stabilize the fabric before cutting to size so the tricot covers the entire piece. Bonus: It also stops the knit from curling!

Notions are such an important part of quilting, so always treat yourself to the best tools and fabrics when it's quilting time.

I hope the tips and tricks in this pocket guide have inspired you to love your sewing space and your sewing time!